REFLECTION

A Collection of Poems by
Anna Claire

A.H. STOCKWELL
PUBLISHERS SINCE 1898

Published in 2023 by
Anna Claire
in association with
Arthur H Stockwell Ltd
West Wing Studios
Unit 166, The Mall
Luton, Bedfordshire
ahstockwell.co.uk

British Library Cataloguing-in-Publication Data
A catalogue record for this book is
available from the British Library.
ISBN: 9780722352984

*The views and opinions expressed herein
belong to the author and do not necessarily
reflect those of AH Stockwell*

*To my sons and grandchildren
and in loving memory of my parents,
Irene and Idris.*

To My Mother, Irene

Mum, best friend, Irene,
Strong and true,
Always available to talk through difficulties,
Discuss problems and share good times.
A helping hand,
A caring heart,
A heart that loves her family—
Husband, children, grandchildren,
Great grandchildren too!

A busy life
Raising a family,
Teaching, baking, gardening,
Sewing,
Knitting also!
Never idle.
Illness has of late,
Taken its toll on your body,
But not your mind.
Your spirit,
Still strong and true.
A heart, softly beating,
Bringing love, not despair,
To us all.
God bless you, Mum,
Thank you for everything,
I love you.
Your daughter,
Anna – Pauline

Contents

Spain 1
The Fishing Village. 2
Silver Birch 3
The Eagle 4
The Storm. 5
The Colour of Love. 6
Text Love 8
The List 9
True Love. 10
Cinders 13
Amour 14
Depths 15
The Proposal 16
Crystal 17
Devotion 18
Marriage 19
Dreams 20
China Doll 21
Heartbreak 22
Teardrops 23
Letter to Heaven 24
The Unborn Baby. 25
Lucy 26
Chinese Girl 27
Fishnet Stockings. 28
Oppression 29
I'm Fat 30
The Christmas Party 32
The Junkie 33
The Junkie's Child 34
Ale 36

Contents (cont.)

Breach of the Peace. 38

There's Nowt Wrong Wi' It. 40

Gentle Passing 41

Live for Today 42

Randell, Ride In Peace 43

Conflict. .44

Air Ambulance 46

The Accident 48

Nadia Leona 51

The Gift. .52

Despair 54

The Funeral 55

Difficulties 56

Celebrate .58

REFLECTION

Spain

Sunlight pouring from the heavens,
Dancing on the sea,
Joyful children playing,
Barefoot on the sand.

Peaceful, dreamy moonlight,
People in the square,
Chatting, laughing, joking,
Happy to be there.
Precious golden moments.

Angels sweetly singing,
Amour in the air,
Couples linking arms,
Sharing tender whispers,
Soft smiles upon their lips.

In every passing minute,
Memories are made,
Thankful for these days,
Reflections of our dreams.

Never be forgotten,
Always in our hearts,
Spain and Spanish warmth,
Kindness gently offered,
Gratefully received.

The Fishing Village

Lush, green leaves,
Swaying palms,
Orange trees, fragrant blossom
Fills a sleepy courtyard.
Showy flowers, red and yellow,
Brightly contrast
Whitewashed homes.

Golden beaches, crystal water
Reflects a light-blue sky.
On fishing boats
Out at sea
Bronzed men work,
Muscles rippling,
Pulling, tugging on fishing nets,
A healthy catch,
Families to feed.

Ladies strolling,
Sitting, resting,
Sipping coffee
Whilst children play.
Dominoes
In outdoor cafés:
Old men quarrel.
Who is winning?

Parasols:
Shade is welcome
From the heat
Of midday sun.
Neighbours, strangers,
Chat and laugh,
Carefree in the summer sun.

Silver Birch

Standing by the shore,
Gracious silver tree.
Catkins fall
Like lambs' tails.
Daffodils
Around you bloom.

Summertime,
Your delicate leaves
Offer shade
As children play,
Paddling in the water,
Resting by the lake.

In time,
Your leaves
Turn yellow,
Reflect the autumn sun,
Golden, diamond shapes
Rustling in the breeze.

Winter comes.
Beautiful silver tree,
You are clothed
In frost and snowflakes,
Sparkling in the sun,
And mirrored
In the water
A dazzling
Crystal tree.

The Eagle

Strong, powerful
Bird of prey,
Admired and feared—
Hunter of the sky!
Soaring, swooping.
Free to glide
Wherever you please,
Across boundaries—
No restrictions,
Limits or rules,
Just freedom
And space
Where time
Is your own.
Graceful, majestic
Bird of prey,
I wish I was
An eagle,
Flying high
With you.

The Storm

Clouds thicken, threaten.
Deep, dark grey.
Fear reigns
As,
Reflecting his mood,
Angry, rumbling,
Thor rages
In a thunderstorm.
Flashes of light
Tear through the sky.
More claps of thunder,
Then
Thor's fury ceases.
His mood calmer,
Clouds part,
Revealing a clear blue sky,
Bringing
Peace on Earth
Once more.

The Colour of Love

Colours make
Our world
A beautiful place.
Subtle shades,
Vivid contrasts—
Brown, black
And white.
Or a mixture—
Coffee-coloured!
Fair, dark,
Tanned,
The colour
Of our skin,
Attractive to us,
Visually,
Sensually.
Warm to the touch,
Welcoming caress.
Our skin—
There for all to see.

Under our skin
Are our feelings,
Who we are,
How we feel,
How we love.

Feelings,
Though unseen,
Still true.
Don't care
About colour—
Brown, black
Or white.
Love comes
In many colours—
All shades.
Love doesn't see
The colour
Of the skin,
But the person
Within.

Text Love

Dim lights, smoke machine.
Dazed looks in a
Peppermint haze.
Couples dance,
Music blasts!
Man meets woman.
Tall, dark stranger
Observes
Pale-blue jeans
And matching bra!
Introductions,
A mobile number!
And so begins
A friendship.
Not actual,
But virtual.
Modern romance—
Text love!
Dreams,
Imagination,
And fantasy.
Not actual,
But
Virtual closeness,
Hugs and kisses.

Busy lives,
Attitudes, outlook,
Keep the couple
Apart.

A virtual couple,
With longings
For an
Actual relationship,
Real closeness,
Hugs and kisses.

The List

Seeking love and
Companionship,
But
A list he writes!
She must not smoke.
Drink?
Only in modest amounts.
Be agile and free.
Work hard,
And independent be.
Own a house,
A car also—
Mobility is a must!
No children,
Neither boy nor girl,
No ties, no pets—
Nothing at all!

Since circumstances can,
And often do,
Rapidly change,
Yet character,
Be it good or bad,
Rarely does.
In search
Of happiness,
Perhaps
It would be wise
To keep an open mind,
Willing to accept,
And
A heart that is
Loving and kind.

True Love

A branch cracks,
Breaks,
A husband falls,
Crashes down
To the ground
Onto his back.
The rope swing
In place
For his children
To enjoy,
But his back
Broken.
Spinal cord
Severed.
A young man
Paralysed.
His life,
His future?
After months
In hospital,
A wheelchair.
His wife
Devastated,
But loyal,
True and
Loving.
Chopped bananas,
Fed them him
As he lay
Flat.
With recovery,
She helped him
Dress.

The children,
As all children,
Argued at first:
"Who will
Push the chair?"
The husband
Returned
To a home
Filled with love.
A happy wife,
Her husband
Alive.
His body broken,
But not his
Spirit.
His face
Full of smiles,
Her heart
Filled with love.
Love—
What is love?
A moment
Of physical pleasure?
No!
Love reaches
To the depths
Of the soul.

Love overcomes
Difficulty.
Love loves
Regardless
Of physical
Disability,
Illness.
Love is
Patient.
Love is
Kind
And makes
Our world
A happier place.
Without love
There is
Nothing,
Just Emptiness.

Cinders

Clothed in rags, a dress
Multi-patched,
She brushes golden curls
From her forehead,
A brow smeared
With soot from fair hands.
She kneels by the hearth,
Tiles cold and black,
Cleans the grate,
Sweeps ashes, cinders remaining
From the glow
Of the previous evening,
The night of the ball—
A ball she attended
Wearing flowing silk gown
And a string of pearls—
Pearls that reflected
Her lustrous young skin.
She danced with her prince
Beneath crystal chandeliers
And a ceiling of stars.
At midnight,
The spell broken
With the chimes of a clock,
She ran,
Leaving behind
A sparkling glass slipper.

Amour

An apple,
Red, delicious,
Tempting.
An alluring smile,
Woman gazing
Lovingly
Towards man.
Enticing,
Leading astray,
Leaving Eden,
Innocence
And Paradise.

Sensual, erotic,
Arousing feelings,
Emotions, desires.
Racing hearts
Beating
In unison,
Eve
Wraps her limbs
Around Adam,
Their lips touch.
Left breathless,
In a passionate
Embrace,
His virile body
Responds
To her warmth,
Her softness,
As their bodies
Become one.

Depths

Youthful faces,
New emotions,
Confusing, exciting,
Silent gazes, soft whispers,
Breathless.
Embrace love's intense moment,
A fleeting memory in time.

Gentle touches, warm smiles,
Loving caresses.
Future promises,
Wedding bells, golden bands.
Babies, young infants follow.
A lasting moment in time.

A perfect vision,
One reflects the other,
Encircling,
United, harmonious,
Peaceful depths of understanding.
The complete
Purity of love,
Eternal, entwined,
Lasting forever
For all time.

The Proposal

Where have you
Been all my life?
My calamitous life,
But 'twas ever thus!
Turbulent, troubled.
You are beautiful,
Intelligent,
Gracious, warm
And loving too.
I hold you
In very high regard.
Would you do me
The honour
Of becoming my wife?
Darling,
Will you marry me?

Crystal

A crystal vase
Held a single rose,
Perfect, beautiful.
Gentle melodies,
Waves lapping on the shore,
Candles offered soft light—
Light that enhanced
Flaxen hair
Which fell across her face
Hiding topaz-blue eyes
But not
An upturned nose.

Across the table, a man—
Her man—
A tender gaze
From deep-brown eyes.
His dark hand
Touches hers, soft and fair.
He held to his lips
And tenderly kissed
Her sparkling diamond,
The crystal vase
Every facet of light
Reflected
Clusters of stars.

Devotion

I love you
With all my heart.
My soul reaches out
To touch yours.
With arms outstretched
I come to you.
Through smiles and tears
I'm there for you,
Always and forever.

All that I am
I give to you.
All that you are
I love, I honour.
Time spent apart,
I miss you;
Moments together
I cherish.
Devoted and true,
I love you
Always and forever.

Marriage

Soft, silver hair,
Warm, tender smiles,
A couple
In their eighties
Shared many happy days.
Sixty years of marriage.
The wife,
She laughed,
Her face still young,
Skin
Clear and fair.
Her secret?
No creams, salons,
Nor expensive beauty treatments,
But love,
Laughter and smiles,
And a passion
For dance,
Movement, activity.
Her husband,
His face lit up,
Blue eyes sparkled
As he remembered
Their youth.
He'd walk for miles
To meet his beloved.
And now?
He loves her still,
Just wishes
He could keep
Up with her
When she dances!

Dreams

I close my eyes
At night,
Weary from the toils
Of day,
And dream!

I dream
We are together.
Hand in hand
We walk
Through shady woods,
Sharing tender moments,
Smiling.

But soon – too soon—
Pale light.
A summer dawn arrives.
Sunlight awakens me.
I leave my dreams
Reluctantly,
To arise
And
Face yet another day
Of reality,
Alone.

China Doll

Lady,
Golden princess,
Dancing all alone,
A mask of smiles,
Hidden tears
As you ponder
Many sorrows.
Outwardly, a woman,
Determined, strong and true,
Yet inside
Like porcelain,
Fragile, delicate, crumbling.
Your heart
Is slowly breaking,
Just like
A china doll.

Heartbreak

Love is
How I felt
When I saw you,
Touched you.
Now all
I have
Is a photo
I kiss
Before
I sleep.
Love is
How I feel
Now,
Empty, alone.
Love is
You.

Teardrops

Sitting quietly, alone,
Eyes lowered,
Lashes brush a face
Pale and sorrowful.
She rests on a slender hand.
Pensive,
Thoughts far away,
Another time, another place,
Remembering,
Smiling tenderly,
Teardrops
Trickle down
Warm peachy cheeks.

She raises her eyes
And looks,
Gazing at the window.
Raindrops sparkle,
Cascade down shining glass.
Rising,
She walks across the room,
Observing a vision
Of the outside world:
Pure-white angels,
Perhaps snowdrops,
Shivering, trembling
Amidst soft melting snow.

Letter to Heaven

I lay my head
Upon the pillow,
Gaze across and see
A photograph of you
Looking lovingly at me.

I close my eyes
And see you—
Beautiful, carefree,
Smiling, laughing happily,
Splashing in the sea.

I feel your warmth,
Your tenderness,
The love I miss so much.
You were taken
From my arms
To live
In Heaven above.

I think of you,
Speak of you,
And would like
So much to say,
"Dear Jill,
I love you still,
And
I always, always will."

The Unborn Baby

My life lost,
Over
Before it began.
I thought I was safe,
Warm and secure
Within my mother's womb.
My tiny heart beating,
Eyes and ears forming,
Limb buds developing,
Growing and moving
Day by day.

My father had left;
My mother decided
It was best—
Best for whom?
Not me!—
To take my life.
She had no support,
Left alone
To decide
My fate.

I have no voice,
But I'm alive.
The result,
Not of love,
But lust.

Mother packed her bag,
Booked a cab
And entered the clinic.
The doctor,
Trained at school
To save most lives,
Took mine.
My life is now over
Before it began.

Lucy

I'm Lucy,
Small in stature,
Blue slanting eyes
And long, fair hair.
I'm clumsy, slow.
Although in school
I find it hard
To read and write,
I do try.

I'm fun, I laugh,
I love and hug.
Sometimes I'm angry.
I shout,
Throw tantrums—
In school,
In shops,
At home.
But mostly
I smile
And love.

I'm Lucy.
Accept me
As I am.
It's not my fault—
No one's to blame.
I was born
With one
Extra chromosome.

Chinese Girl

Two babies born:
A little boy,
A tiny girl.
The boy,
Cherished, loved,
Accepted,
Wrapped in blue,
The colour of princes,
Of the gods.
A little emperor.
A dream come true
As parents glow with pride.

A tiny girl,
Unwanted, unloved,
Discarded.
Left alone,
Wrapped in rags.
Placed in a crib
With many other babies,
All girls,
No parent's tender touch,
No love,
Care or concern.

Alone
To whimper and cry
And slowly die.
To starve.
Why?

She was a girl—
A beautiful
Chinese baby girl.

Fishnet Stockings

A young girl,
Mid-teens,
Walks the streets
Alone,
In the dark.
Fishnet stockings,
Short skirts
And boots.
She
Stands on corners,
Waiting
For a man—
Any man—
To stop.
She lives,
Not with her family,
But in a group of girls—
Young girls—
Influenced
By
An older man
Who says he cares.
Cares?
Not for the girls,
Their welfare
Nor their future,
But for himself,
His bank balance
And his own
Selfish desires.
For this
He risks
The lives,
Health
And well-being
Of these vulnerable
Young girls.

Oppression

The smiles,
Sparkle, laughter,
Gone.
Alone, silent,
In a corner
She sits.
Her face
Drawn,
Tear-stained.
Intimidated,
Threatened,
Bullied.
A victim
Of cowards.

Lift up
Your face,
Stand firm,
Strong.
Face the
Bullies,
The cowards,
With courage,
Confidence,
And
Smile
Once more.

I'm Fat

I gaze in the mirror;
My reflection stares back.
Fat, large,
Obese.
I'm fourteen,
Slender, blonde,
Beautiful,
So people say.
Slender?
I see fat.
Beautiful?
No, I'm ugly.
I must not eat.
I will slim,
Diet,
Eat just
One yogurt
A day—
No more.
More
And I'll be
Grotesque.

My mother pleads,
"Just eat this banana,
Kerry, please!"
We visit the doctor,
The dietician.
They offer advice,
Support,
Name my 'condition'
Anorexia nervosa.
I don't understand
My mother's tears.
Can she not see
How fat I am?
When will she realise
I must not eat;
I must diet.
Then I'll be
Beautiful,
Like Kelly,
Tall, slender,
Stunning.

The Christmas Party

Fun, frivolity,
Laughter.
Wine flowing
As colleagues
Celebrate.
A festive party.

The music begins.
Let's dance.
Sway, move
To the beat.
In jovial mood
The boss
Joins in,
Mingles with
His staff.

His brain
Soaked
In ale,
He wears
Not a Santa hat,
As one would expect,
But a lampshade—
And, of course,
It is pink!

The Junkie

Time for the fix.
Finding the vein,
Injecting.
Chasing the dragon.
Sniffing, snorting,
Tension released.
Gazing, staring.
Vacant looks,
Blank faces.
Dosed with dope,
High
Minds floating, drifting.
Time goes fast.
Images sail slowly
Through the brain.
Visions,
Dreamy, blurred.
Angels, devils,
In the mind.
Unaware of
The world around.
The kids?
What kids?
Do I have kids?
I can't remember.
Maybe; maybe not.
Drifting, dreaming,
Sinking slowly,
Everything is slow,
Falling
Into another world—
A world apart—
A world where
Care and trouble
Do not exist,
At least for
The duration
Of the fix.

The Junkie's Child

My mother,
She loves me
When she's aware.
Sometimes she injects—
Heroin, I think.
She drifts away,
Leaves this world,
Enters another,
So far away
I cannot reach her.
I cope – I must.
I help my mother,
Dress baby sister,
Make breakfast
Then leave for school.
Alone.

I worry—
I'm concerned
For my sister.
What can I do?
How can I learn,
Concentrate on lessons,
Thinking of home,
Of mother
In a trance?
And baby
Crawling around
The flat,
Alone?
I am a child.

For me,
No carefree childhood,
No laughter,
Fun and games.
Only responsibility,
Troubles and concerns
As
My mother
Takes drugs.

Ale

A mother,
Young and fair,
Two babies,
Still in nappies,
Used to a
Life
Of fun,
Of parties,
Drink
And boyfriends.
She turns away
From responsibility,
The daily chores
Of wife
And mother,
And drinks
Bottle
After bottle
Of wine
And ale.
Her husband,
The babies' father,
Saddened
By her behaviour,
Left work
And stayed at home
To care
For his wife
And little babes.

One day,
The mother
Left home
In a drunken
Stupor
With her boyfriend
To attend
A party.
She
Never returned.
The father,
Left alone
To raise
His two
Little ones.

Breach of the Peace

Sunday morning,
The early hours,
Nightclubs
Close their doors.
Young men, young women,
Teenagers,
Drunk,
Wander onto the streets.
A young man staggers.
A girl trips up—
Her head hits the ground,
Blood pouring down
Her face.
A crowd surrounds,
Push and shove,
A scuffle,
A fight breaks out.
Bottles smashed,
Broken glass,
Cuts and bruises,
More blood.
Someone calls the police,
The ambulance.
Flashing lights,
Sirens.

Paramedics
Rush forward,
Comfort the girl,
Take her to hospital.
A young man's arrested,
And then another,
Both driven off
By car,
Lights flashing,
To the station—
The police station—
After another
Good night
On the town!

There's Nowt Wrong Wi' It

"Will yer put
That back on't shelf?
There's nowt wrong
Wi' it."
What language
Is this?
English?
No, 'tis Lancashire!
'Tis proud.
'Tis down to earth.
'Tis incomprehensible,
But interesting!
Adds richness
And character,
But often brings
Prejudice.
How should
One speak?
Clearly, precisely—
"Would you place
That product back
On the shelf, please?
It is
In good condition
For sale."
Or
From one's roots,
With honesty
And pride?

Gentle Passing

Little cat, sick and tired,
Weary of this world.
We tried so hard
To save your life,
The veterinary surgeon and I.
Tests and medication,
And further tests.
We fought and prayed
To no avail.

Your little body,
Your gentle spirit,
Giving up the fight.
Your pain was great,
So we decided
To help you on your way.
I held you close;
You felt a needle,
Then your soft body
Leant gently
Beside me,
Sweet Lydia,
As you quietly
Slipped away.

Live for Today

Diagnosis cancer!
Stunned, shocked silence.
Disbelief – how can this be?
Why us?
Shocked into silence,
Inwardly screaming.
Hope? No hope.
The future is taken away,
Snatched from us
By one word:
Terminal.
Another: *inoperable*.

How can we live?
How should we live?
Live for today!
Grasp at life.
Share special moments.
Don't think of tomorrow,
The pain, the sorrow.
Whatever you do,
Do now,
Today.
Have fun, laugh,
See, feel.
Ride rollercoasters!

Live every moment—
Don't wait till tomorrow.
Do what you can;
Say what you must,
Right now.
Tomorrow
May never come.

Randell, Ride In Peace

Newquay,
The cry of gulls,
Waves curling, spraying,
Lashing against
Rugged rocks
Of cold steel grey...
The fierce roar,
Angry, unrelenting, deafening
As the sound of the lion
Guarding his territory,
His eyes shining, gleaming,
Golden.
Sun setting,
Harbour lights reflect the hostile sea.
Ferries carry home men,
Eyes glazed from local brew.
Swaying, slurring.
Seeing
Phantom surfers rise,
Like phoenix, from beneath,
And ride the waves.
Youthful ghosts from days
Gone by,
Visions under moonlit skies,
Here, then gone,
Vanished from our view.
Randell,
Ride in peace.

Conflict

Bombs falling, explosions light up the sky.
Destruction, dust, death,
All in the name of freedom.
Families shattered:
Children without fathers, mothers without sons,
Innocence caught up in the conflict.
Children lie dead, hastily buried.
Whose children were they?
Boys and girls with broken bodies,
Limbs blasted off, severely burnt.
A child, a boy, with no arms,
No hands to wipe away his tears.
His family all dead.
A girl, bandaged, burnt, pleading for help,
No medicine available.
The doctors, so sad, look on,
Unable to ease her pain.
Mothers weep and wail and beat their breasts—
The breasts that once nourished their child.
Their faces stricken with grief.
Fathers in sorrow – deep sorrow—
Dig with their bare hands in shallow graves,
Searching, searching for the face of their child.
Tears, prayers—
They need to know
Where their child lies dead.

They need to bury their child with dignity.
They need to visit, to remember
Cherished memories of an innocent lost.
Is this the price of freedom?
These parents have no freedom—
No freedom from grief or sorrow.
Their lives shattered, their hearts broken.
When will they find peace?
They reach out their arms:
"Please help me!"
How I long to reach back to them,
But I can't.
They are thousands of miles from England,
In Iraq.

Air Ambulance

The road, straight, flat.
The car, sporty, fast,
Deep red in colour, like blood.
Speeding, racing.
Suddenly, unexpectedly,
A bend.
Screeching, swerving,
Losing control.
A failed attempt to avoid
An oncoming car.
Crash, crunch,
Bent metal crumbles.
Airbags inflate.
Drivers sit still,
Slumped, silent,
Unconscious.
Bruises, cuts,
Deep-red dripping blood
And silence.

A passing motorist stops,
Shocked, shaking,
Reaches for his phone
And calls,
"Urgent, urgent,
Serious accident—
Air ambulance is needed
NOW!"
Details follow.

Moments later,
Sirens, blue lights
Flashing,
Police arrive at the scene.
Above, in the air,
Swooping, soaring,
The wings of an eagle?
No!
Blades rotating.
The rumbling
Sound of an engine.
A helicopter appears,
Air ambulance arrives,
Lands close to the scene,
No time to lose—
Lives to be saved.
Crew members make haste,
Tend the victims,
In critical condition,
Emergency care,
Resuscitation.
Placed on stretchers
Then
Board the air ambulance
And race through the sky
To the closest
Trauma unit,
Accident and emergency,
Only minutes away.

The Accident

Sunday afternoon,
A glorious day
In early spring.
A mother, her partner
And her son,
Jonathan,
Drive through
The countryside,
Looking forward
To enjoying
Their picnic.

A bend, a motorcyclist
Speeding, racing
At top speed.
He brakes,
Skids
Then crashes,
Hitting the car.
He is thrown
In the air,
Killed instantly.

The driver
Of the car
Shakes, trembles,
Alive.
His partner
Dead beside him.
Her son,
Nine years old,
His dog still
Curled up
On his knee,
Both dead.
Dear child,
Only yesterday
I saw you,
Laughing, playing,
Full of life.
And now—
Your life ended,
So tragically,
Needlessly—
The result
Of a road traffic accident.
A victim of speed.

How can I tell
My son
Away on camp?
He phoned:
"Is all well?"
He asked.
"Of course,"
I replied,
As I decided
To break the news
Upon his return.

The boy,
He was
An only child.
His father,
Devastated,
Visited his son,
Lying 'asleep'
In his coffin.
Peaceful,
Lifeless.
His father,
Lovingly,
Spiked his hair.

"I'm sorry
I wouldn't
Let you
Spike your hair,
Son,"
He said,
Tears rolling
Down his cheeks.
Then he left
His son,
Lying alone,
Lifeless,
In his coffin.
Killed
By speed!

Nadia Leona

Nadia quietly packed her case.
She must go,
Leave this cruel man
And the chains of abuse.
His charm,
Shown to the outside world,
Vanishes as he steps through the door
Of his property, not a family home.

A spirited lioness,
She raised her sons,
Showing courage and love
As each boy became man.

Now Nadia, pale and drawn,
Years of neglect
Have damaged her soul.
She must go!
Embrace freedom
With open arms.
A future uncertain,
But Nadia Leona
Smiles
As she leaves
With hope in her heart.

The Gift

Marie walked,
Slowly,
Quietly,
Into the church,
Her eyes lowered.
Tears rolled
Down her cheeks.
Her son lay
In a hospital bed.
Fatally injured.

She walked
Down the aisle,
Gazed up
At the statue
Of a saint,
Lighted candles
Flickering
At its feet.

She held a candle,
Lit it,
And prayed
For the life
Of her son.
She implored God
To help her,
Then she turned,
Left the church
And wandered
Through the city,
Aimlessly
Making her way
To the hospital
Where her son lay.

She stared down
At his young body
With a sorrowful look,
Eyes shining
With teardrops,
And gently kissed
His cheek
As his life
Quietly ended.

As he breathed
His last,
God's presence felt,
She promised
His organs to others.
In death,
In sorrow,
A gift of life,
Of hope,
Brought comfort
To her
As tears
Rolled
Down her face.

Despair

So sorry,
I must leave you now.
I am tired of life.
I cannot live.

Everything goes wrong.
I cannot sleep.
I am so unhappy.
No friends to care,
People laugh and stare.
I'm so alone
Since my love left me.
Tell her I love her still.

I truly hope
My family will not
Be ashamed of me.
So sorry
To be
A failure in life.

I won't miss this world;
I'm sure it will not miss me.
I hope to find happiness
In a better place.

Goodbye, my family.
With all my heart
And soul
I love you.
I will always
Be with you,
Watching you,
Guiding you,
From
That better place.

The Funeral

Above,
Glorious summer sky.
Below,
People in black, in sorrow,
Silent, shocked.
Tear-stained faces,
Bodies shaking with grief.
The reason?
The death,
Sudden and tragic,
Of a young man,
Just twenty-one.
The cause?
Too terrible
To contemplate.
He died
Alone,
Depressed,
In utter despair.
The way he died
Explains the intense grief,
The deep sorrow,
The tragedy.

Difficulties

Difficulties,
Placed before us,
To try us,
Test us,
Make us strong.

Problems
To be overcome,
Make us fight,
Battle through
And win.

Is there any
Remover
Of difficulties?
For those
With faith
There is.

God listens,
Gives hope,
Feels compassion
For His
Humble servants
On Earth.

He shows the way,
Guides us
Through this
Darkness,
Sadness
And despair,
Leads us
To a
Shining light
Of hope
And love.

Verily,
If we abide
By the will
Of God
Peace
Rests
In our hearts.

Celebrate

One day,
When I leave
This world,
Do not grieve,
No sadness, sorrow show;
Be joyful,
Celebrate my life.

No tears to flow,
No dark,
Depressing clothes,
But bright and cheerful
Colours
Please do wear.

And flowers?
Not lilies,
But roses
Of any,
Every hue.

www.ingramcontent.com/pod-product-compliance
Lightning Source LLC
LaVergne TN
LVHW041208080426
835508LV00008B/853